I HAVE EPILEPSY, AND IT'S OKAY!

Written by
Dr. William M. Bauer

Illustrated by
Mallory Hill

WestBow Press books may be ordered through booksellers or by contacting:

WestBow Press
A Division of Thomas Nelson & Zondervan
1663 Liberty Drive
Bloomington, IN 47403
www.westbowpress.com
844-714-3454

Interior Image Credit: Mallory Hill

ISBN: 978-1-6642-4342-2 (sc)
ISBN: 978-1-6642-4343-9 (e)

Library of Congress Control Number: 2021912589

Print information available on the last page.

WestBow Press rev. date: 09/13/2021

WESTBOW PRESS®
A DIVISION OF THOMAS NELSON & ZONDERVAN

I HAVE EPILEPSY, AND
IT'S OKAY!

IT'S OKAY!
YOU GOT THIS!
YOU ARE ENOUGH!
YOU ARE AWESOME!!

IT'S OKAY!
YOU CAN DO IT!
I'M SO PROUD OF YOU!
EVERYTHING WILL BE OKAY!
DO GREAT THINGS!
YOU GOT IT!
IT'S OKAY
STOP

About the Author:

Dr. William M. (Bill) Bauer is a licensed clinical counselor in the rural Mid-Ohio Valley area who was a former classroom teacher, principal, and college professor. He has worked with children and adults with disabilities all of his life and hopes that this book brings an understanding to children with disabilities, their teachers, and their classmates. Dr. Bauer was born with a severe hearing impairment.

THIS BOOK IS DEDICATED TO:

ALL PEOPLE WITH DISABILITIES WHOSE LIVES ARE SHARED IN THIS BOOK SERIES TO MAKE THE WORLD A BETTER PLACE. ALL WE WANT IS TO BE ACCEPTED AS WE ARE, HAVE FRIENDS, LIVE IN OUR COMMUNITIES AND TO DREAM AS OUR NON-DISABLED PEERS.

SPECIAL THANKS TO MY WIFE, MARY ELLA, DAUGHTER MADISON RYSER, HER HUSBAND ANDREW AND GRANDSON JACK.

#GRANTSPEED.
LOVE YOU, SON

To:

From:

Forewords:

I have had the pleasure of working with Dr. Bauer in the professional education and mental health fields for over two decades, and this book series is his latest outstanding work to help young people understand and accept differences. Each title focuses on a uniqueness and assures us that "it is OKAY!"

Dr. Stephanie Starcher
Public School Superintendent

Being different is OK! Every effort to erase stigma surrounding our differences is important. The earlier we start, the better chance we have at preventing stigma from even occurring. I had the honor of meeting Dr. Bill Bauer when I was in college, and it is no surprise his work as a mental health advocate would transpire into this series of books. I'm thankful for his commitment to celebrating our differences.

Nick Gehlfuss, MFA, Actor, film and television.
Currently, Dr. Halstead, Chicago Med.

This book series by Dr. William Bauer – my good friend Bill – fills a niche in children's literature that embraces diversity and self esteem. This series is not only important, but extremely fun. As founder of Orphans International, I look forward to reading these stories to children of all faiths and abilities around the world. This book is indeed a living testament to Bill's own son. The world is a better place because of Bill Bauer! #GrantSpeed

James Jay Dudley Luce, Founder Orphans International Worldwide,
International Entrepreneur

MY NAME IS PHILLIP, I HAVE EPILEPSY, AND IT'S OKAY!

EPILEPSY IS SOMETHING THAT I HAVE LIVED WITH SINCE I WAS A BABY.

1 2
3 4
5 6
7 8
9 10
A
B
C

THE BRAIN MAKES US DO DIFFERENT THINGS. IT CAN CAUSE US TO HAVE SEIZURES.

SOME PEOPLE WITH EPILEPSY STARE INTO "SPACE;" SOME SHAKE A LITTLE; SOME SHAKE A LOT. EPILEPSY CAUSES SOME OF US TO SLEEP, AND WE DON T KNOW WHAT IS HAPPENING. THESE ARE CALLED SEIZURES. I HAVE THE KIND THAT MAKES MY BODY SHAKE, AND I HAVE TO LIE DOWN.

IT CAN BE SCARY FOR SOMEONE TO SEE. THEY ARE USUALLY CONTROLLED BY TAKING THE MEDICINE MY DOCTOR GIVES ME. AT TIMES I NEVER KNOW WHEN I AM GOING TO HAVE A SEIZURE, BUT I KNOW WHEN I DO, I WILL BE OKAY WHEN IT'S OVER.

BEFORE SCHOOL STARTS, MY MOM AND DAD MEET WITH MY TEACHERS AND SCHOOL NURSE TO TELL HER WHAT MEDICINE I TAKE AND WHAT TO EXPECT. THEY EVEN TALK TO MY CLASSMATES (I DO TOO) ABOUT MY SEIZURES SO NO ONE WILL BE SCARED.

NURSE'S
OFFICE

ALL OF MY FRIENDS AT SCHOOL KNOW WHAT TO DO WHEN I HAVE A SEIZURE. THEY HELP ME AND DON'T TREAT ME ANY DIFFERENTLY. I LOVE MY FRIENDS WHO HELP ME.

SOMETIMES I FEEL LIKE I AM GOING TO HAVE A SEIZURE. IF I FEEL THIS WAY, I TELL AN ADULT AND THEY KEEP AN EYE ON ME. THIS FEELING IS CALLED AN AURA. IT HELPS ME KNOW WHEN I AM GOING TO HAVE ONE.

EVERYTHING WILL BE JUST FINE.

I DON'T WANT PEOPLE TO KEEP WATCHING OVER ME AND ACTING LIKE I'M GOING TO HAVE A SEIZURE EVERY MINUTE OF EVERYDAY. I WANT TO BE LIKE EVERYONE ELSE.

I CAN'T WAIT TO GROW UP AND GO FOR MY DREAMS!

FUTURE
EXPLORE
DESIGN
VIDEO
GAMES
$
GOALS

MY NAME IS PHILLIP, I HAVE EPILEPSY, AND IT'S OKAY!

Printed in the United States
by Baker & Taylor Publisher Services